My Baby's First Religious Words

An ABC Book for Toddlers from A to Z Introducing them to God and Religious Concepts

For Ages 3-8

BY THE SINCERE SEEKER KIDS COLLECTION

A is for

Almighty : God
is very powerful
and can do
anything! He
created this
whole world and
all the people,
animals , and
plants in it!

B is for Belief : Although we cannot see God, we believe in him and love Him very much!

C is for

charity: we
should always
try to help people
in need.

Charity
Box

D is for Devotion : We show love and respect for God by worshipping Him and doing what He wants us to do.

E is for Earth :

Earth is the place God created for us to live in, along with animals

F is for Forgiveness: we show mercy to others who have wronged us so God shows mercy to us.

H is for Hope: We place our hope in God that He will guide us in this world and reward us with Paradise in the next world for being good.

I is for Inspiration : We encourage others to be good and learn about God.

J is for Jesus Christ : Who God sent as a Prophet to teach his people about God .

K is for Kingdom of Heaven :

A beautiful and fun place where people who believe in God and follow His commands will go after they die

L is for Love: love comes from God. He loves us very much, and we love Him too!

M is for Mary: The mother of Jesus Christ, who was very kind and always did what God asked of her.

N is for Noah:

A Prophet of God who taught his people to worship God alone and built an ark that saved the believers of God and animals from a great flood .

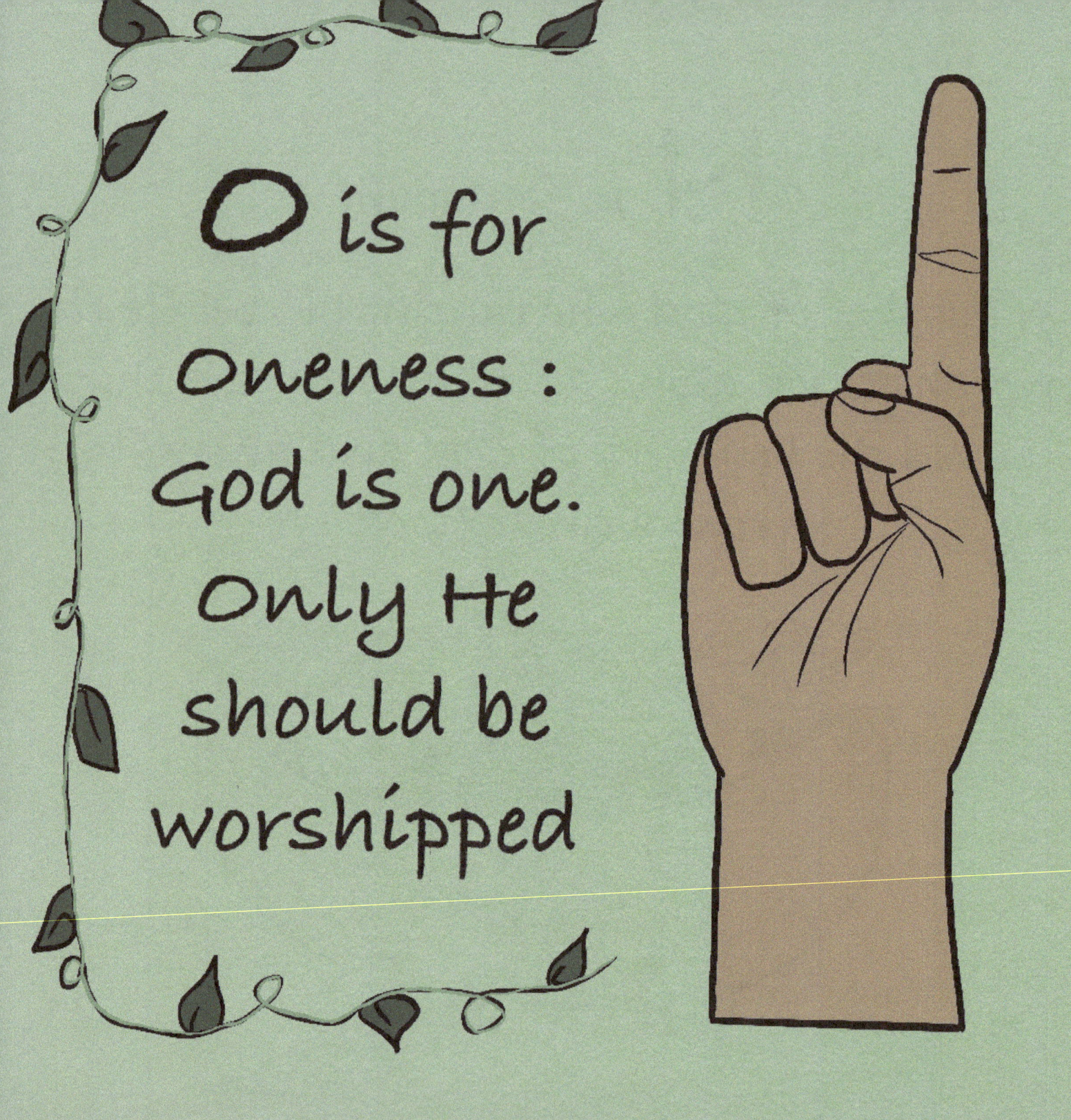

O is for

Oneness :
God is one.
Only He
should be
worshipped

P is for peace: When we believe and worship God, we feel at peace

Q is for Questions : We ask questions about God so we can learn more and become closer to Him.

R is for

Righteousness: Doing what God taught us is good and fair, which includes being kind, honest, and respectful to others .

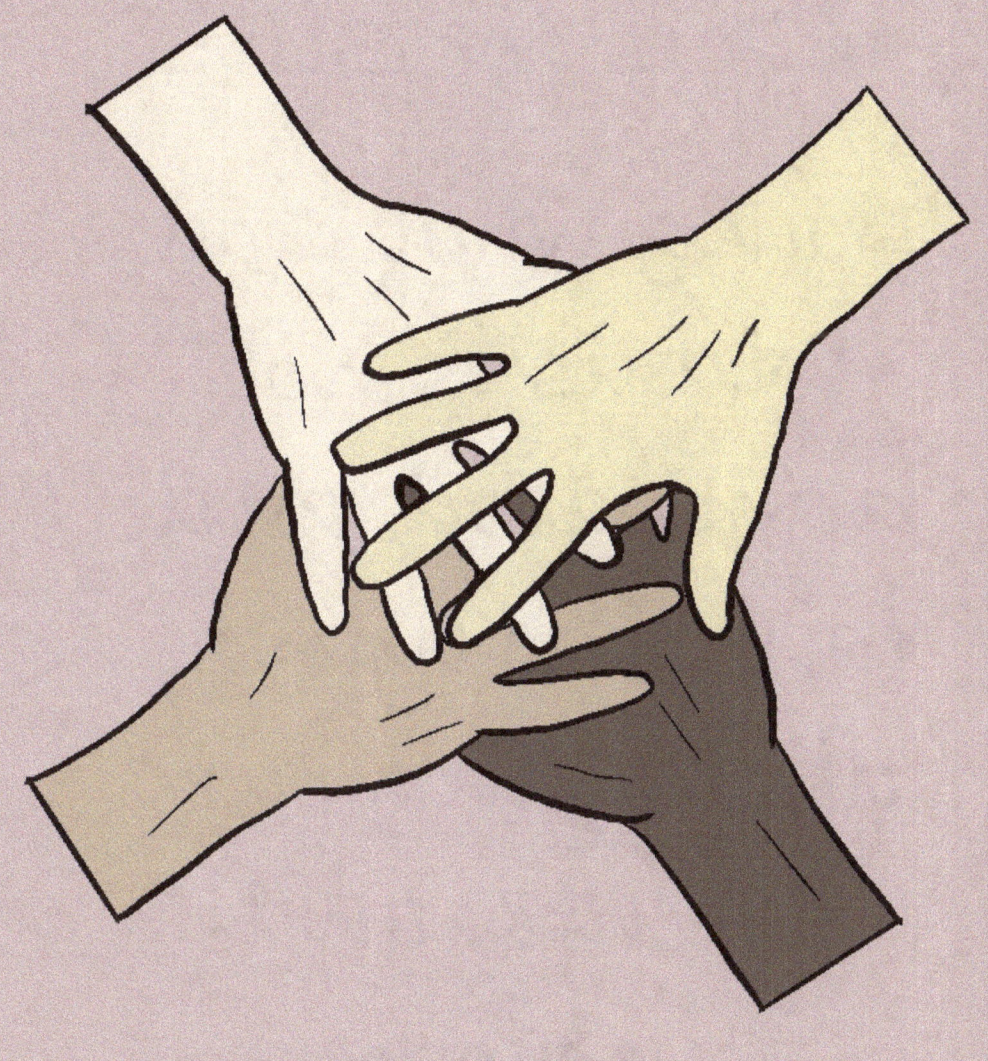

S is for sin:

Doing what God told us is not right, good, and fair, like lying, disobeying our parents, and hurting others .

T is for

Truth: God wants us to always be honest, and not say something that is not true. Being honest is very important and makes God happy.

U is for Unity: God wants us all to come together to worship God and be united in faith and love .

V is for

Victory : Those who believe in God and follows His commands will be among the successful people and enter paradise .

W is for

Worship : We worship God because He is worthy of worship, and we respect and love him .

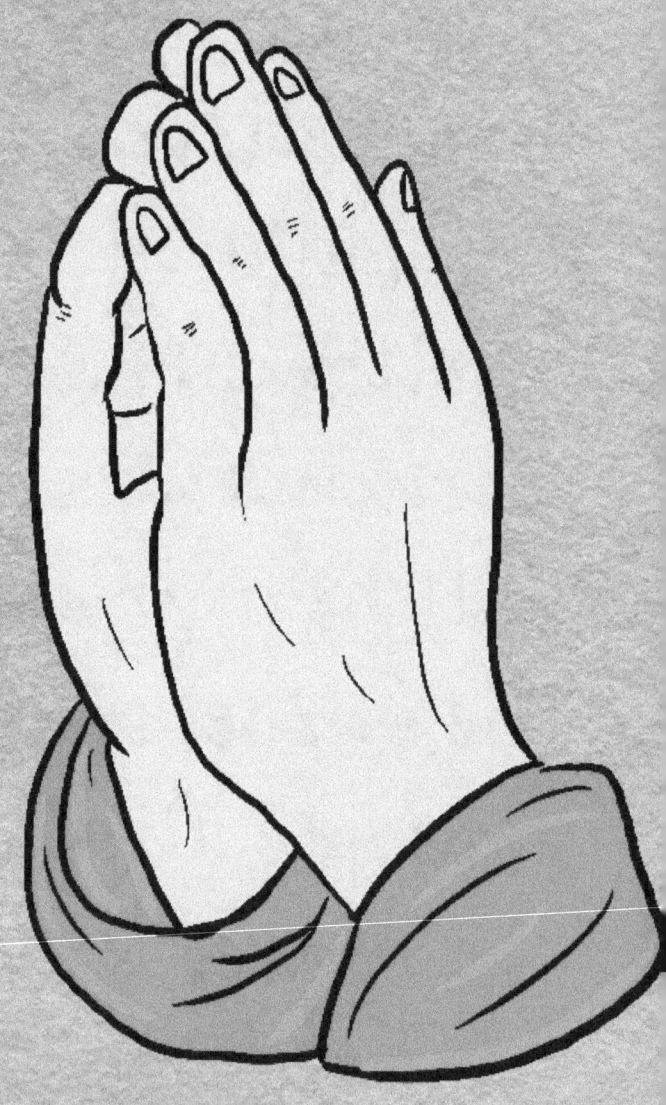

X is for X-Ray: A picture that doctors take of the inside of our bodies, created so amazingly by God to help us stay healthy and strong.

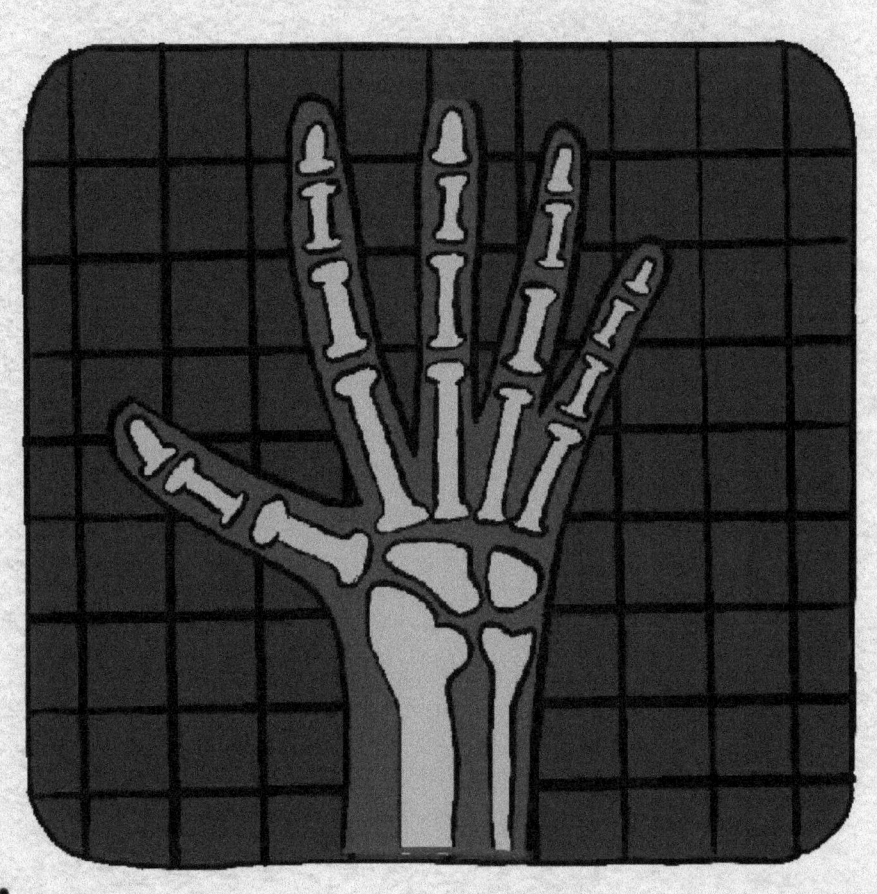

Y is for Yes:

What we say when asked if we believe in God.

Z is for Zoo: A location for God's creatures.